The Way to the TOP is DOWN

By Stan Tyra

Soar with Eagles

A Publisher Driven by Vision and Purpose

The Way to the Top is Down. Copyright © 2006 by Stan Tyra. All rights reserved. No part of this book may be reproduced or transmitted in any form or by any means, electronic or mechanical, including photocopying, recording, or by any information storage and retrieval system, without written permission from the author, except for the inclusion of brief quotations in a review.

Soar with Eagles books may be purchased for educational, business, or sales promotional use. For information, please contact Soar with Eagles.

ISBN-10: 0977140326
ISBN-13: 9780977140329

First Edition

Published by Soar with Eagles
1200 North Mallard Lane
Rogers, AR 72756, USA
www.soarhigher.com

Interior design by Carrie Perrien Smith
Cover design by Julie Curd

Printed in the United States of America

Contents

Introduction vii

1. It All Begins With a Dream............................. 1

2. Living Past the Pain of Rejection 17

3. What's Seducing You?..................................... 25

4. False Accusation Always Hurts 35

5. Detouring Past Disappointment 39

6. Success: The Greatest Test of All 43

7. Jesus: Our Perfect Example............................ 49

8. Downward Mobility: Keys to Greatness 57

vi

Introduction

"Who is wise and understanding among you? He should show his works by good conduct with wisdom's gentleness. But if you have bitter envy and selfish ambition in your heart, don't brag and lie in defiance of the truth. Such wisdom does not come down from above, but is earthly, sensual, demonic. For where envy and selfish ambition exist, there is disorder of every kind of evil. But the wisdom from above is first pure, then peace-loving, gentle, compliant, full of mercy and good fruits, without favoritism and hypocrisy."

James 3:13-17 (Holman Christian Standard Bible)

I remember watching when my children were young. No matter what the activity of the moment was, they seemed to often be yelling, "Me first! I'm first!" or "Mine! That's mine!" While we believed this was mainly a product of immaturity, it is, in fact, the essence of what is evil today — yes, it is still a true mark of immaturity. Children demand, "Feed me, change me, entertain me, pamper me, notice me." Once, the church was so filled with this type of behavior, the Apostle Paul told them to grow up and stop acting like children. Sadly, this childish behavior is lived out by many of our corporate and world leaders still today.

Even more sad for me is hearing Christians who continually yell, "Me first" and "What about me?" Oh, they may not say it out loud, but their actions say it loud enough. It's the drive-through crowd — only interested in what they can get and how quick they can get out of there. They walk in last minute — or late — sit, consume, and walk out until next Sunday.

> *"A nation will be strong and endure when it has intelligent, sensible leaders."*
>
> Proverbs 28:2
> *(The Message)*

I once had a woman tell me it was the church's responsibility to feed her. I quickly reminded her that my four-year-old son could, in fact, feed himself if necessary; only an infant is totally dependent on someone to feed him and perhaps it was time for her to grow up. Needless to say, I wasn't well received. However, many years later, that same woman told me how important I was to her at that time and if she had it to do over, she would do it different. If we only eat once a week physically, we call it either sickness or a fast. If we eat once a week spiritually, we call it revival!

God always wants to raise up great servants who understand that *the way up* is *down*. This new generation of believers adopts an attitude and lives a lifestyle that places their priorities behind those of others. These godly individuals put a greater value on God and others than they do themselves.

"Whoever wants to become great must be a servant to others."

Matthew 20:26 (God's Word Translation)

All of us have the ability to influence people. We are all subject to living this same selfish, self-centered, self-serving life. This book is about descending. It's about giving up our rights for someone else. If you find yourself thinking more about yourself than anyone else, you are on a path to loneliness, isolation, frustration, and contempt for all those around you.

Today, we are all bombarded with images of people falling. Every day it seems that there is another scandal that exposes a leader or group of leaders who somehow came to believe that they were the only ones who mattered.

We find this in our corporate world, the countries of our world, our families and yes, even our churches. During my lifetime, I have seen two presidents fall — Nixon and Clinton. I have seen the Berlin Wall fall, and I have witnessed the toppling of an evil dictator known as Sadam Hussein. I have watched as countless corporations have been exposed and had their leaders fall due to corrupt business practices. As they have fallen, they have plundered the lives of all those who trusted them and looked up to them as their leader.

The stage is set for a new generation of people that excels in godly character. To this new breed of people, character will not be a noble word to toss around; it will be the very essence of who they are. They will be people of character first and everything else will follow.

A great teacher, Dudley Hall, referred to them as the Joseph Generation. Like the Joseph of the Old Testament, they stand every test and serve their way to the top. Once their character has been chiseled and perfected, they will stand with hands full of bread for a famine-struck people. They will not be vindictive but instead full of compassion, love, vision, character, and integrity. There is a famine in our land and God is looking for good life managers.

Currently, there is one crisis right after another; one natural disaster right after another; and major economic crisis throughout the world. Our education system is not working. Marriages and families are not working. Rather than manage, we believe the answer is to throw more money at it or try to legislate it. The country and world is hungry for life. There is a famine in our world — a spiritual famine that has countless millions of people looking for food that will satisfy the hunger.

"For even I didn't come to be served but to serve others and give my life as a ransom for many."

Mark 10:45 (New Living Translation)

"For we are God's workmanship, created in Christ Jesus to do good works, which God prepared in advance for us to do."

Ephesians 2:10 (New International Version)

Through this book, it is my purpose to lay out the steps or "tests" that every Christian who dreams of making a difference must walk through. These steps downward, if taken, will make us greater than anything we might ever do on our own. The scripture tells us that in order to *increase*, we must first *decrease*. Jesus Himself said that He didn't come to *be served* but *to serve*. He must be our example if we are ever to walk in real power that impacts people from a heart of love.

I don't write from a point of view of one who has completed the entire test. There are stages and steps that we all must continue to walk through. However, it would be my hope and my prayer that we might identify and choose a path that is better characterized as "descending into greatness." We will take a look at the life of Joseph and examine the steps he took — or was taken through — to prepare him to be one of the greatest servant-leaders in history.

> *"God has given each of you some <u>special abilities</u>; be sure to use them <u>to help each other</u> ..."*
>
> *1 Peter 4:10*
> *(Living Bible)*

Walk with me now as we learn a new model for effective Christians that we will call the Joseph Generation. There are seven distinctly different life stages or downward steps in his development. Let's take a closer look.

1 It All Begins With a Dream

Did you read the introduction? If not, take a few moments and go back. You will not fully understand the purpose and passion of this book unless you read the introduction.

Are you a dreamer? Do you have a dream that absolutely drives you? Has God said something to you that energizes your life with a sense of purpose?

Most of us have heard Dr. Martin Luther King's speech, "I Have a Dream," delivered August 28, 1963 at the Lincoln Memorial in Washington D.C. It's quite apparent that he, in fact, had a dream that created a passion that drove his activity and energized him every day. It also energized others to act.

As our story opens, we find Joseph in Israel with his family. He's about 17 years old and lives in the town of Hebron. He's living with eleven brothers and one sister. This is the story of dreams and how dreams begin. Joseph is an example of how dreams can cause us to develop. His life is the story of how dreams are realized. It is the story of how you should live your dream once you reach it.

Joseph was the youngest and the weakest. He would have been voted least likely to succeed by the family, a Daddy's boy or the "prized pig" as my friend Drew Tucker refers to himself in his youth. However, God has a way of looking beyond all man can see and recognizing a heart that is humble.

You might ask, "How do I know if I have been called?" Have you responded? Your response will confirm the call. God chooses the weak and foolish to confound the wise.

> "Brothers consider your calling; not many are wise from a human perspective, not many powerful, not many of noble birth. Instead, God has chosen the world's foolish things to shame the wise, and God has chosen the world's weak things to shame the strong. God has chosen the world's insignificant and despised things, the things viewed as nothing, so He might bring to nothing the things that are viewed as something so that no one can

boast in His presence. But from Him you are in Christ Jesus who for us became wisdom from God as well as righteousness, sanctification, and redemption in order that, as it is written: The one who boasts must boast in the Lord."

1 Corinthians 1:26-31
(Holman Christian Standard Bible)

Joseph was a man of vision. He had a sense of destiny. No matter where he was, he couldn't forget he had seen something. Have you seen something that is never far from you? Have you heard the voice of God speak so loudly into your spirit that you cannot get it out of your head or your heart? That's what happened to Joseph. He was never the same. Although maybe untimely, he couldn't stop talking about it. He wanted to tell others what he had seen no matter what it cost him.

There have been two times in my life when God clearly communicated to my heart that He was calling me to a purpose.

When I was a young boy living in Cottondale, Alabama, I would spend the days of summer at my Aunt Peggy's house while Mom and Dad were at work. I was probably around age nine or ten on this particular day. I was riding my bicycle in the woods on an unfamiliar trail.

Suddenly, I came upon a sharp turn — almost 90 degrees it seemed. As many young boys often do, I was riding very fast and feeling quite invincible. However, I could not maneuver this turn. It was too sharp, and I was going too fast. I drove my bike off the embankment.

The small valley below was full of cut timber that had been pushed into the bottom. Sticks, logs, and limbs were sticking up promising severe injury if not death. I believe the small valley was perhaps 20 feet deep and maybe 20 to 30 feet across. I'm not real sure but I just remember it looked like the Grand Canyon at that very moment.

From the time I sailed off the embankment, I don't remember anything else until later — who knows how much time had passed. I woke to find myself lying flat on my back on the upslope of the small valley. I had sailed completely across the timber-filled gorge. When I woke up, I was so at peace that my first thoughts were that I was either dead or paralyzed.

Surprisingly, I didn't have a single pain and as I looked myself over, I realized I didn't have a scratch on me. It was the eeriest feeling but yet I felt totally peaceful at the same time. I sat for a while contemplating how strange it all seemed — it was most surreal.

Next, I noticed that my bike was also lying next to me. It too had no signs of a crash — no scratches or dents anywhere and the handlebars were still straight. It was positioned as if it had been gently placed there. I looked across the gorge and quickly knew that I didn't understand what had happened, but there was no way possible for both me and my bike to fly that distance, land softly beside one another, and not have any damage to show for it.

After I laid there for a while, I picked up my bike, walked out the end of the gorge, and returned to my aunt's house. I never forgot that moment. It was and is still imprinted on my mind and my heart.

Some 20 years later, I was attending a church service with my wife, Debbie, at a local hotel in Little Rock, Arkansas. The church was a new satellite campus of a church out of San Antonio, Texas. Debbie and I had decided to go hear the guest preacher as we had heard him preach at a Bible conference a couple of years prior. It was a great service, and we were blessed and ministered to through the Word and the worship.

As we were leaving, a man walked up to Debbie and I and thanked us for being there. We chatted for a moment and then, in the presence of my wife, he said, "I believe the Lord would have me encourage you that you are not out of His care or His purpose. The Lord wants to remind you that when you were a young boy and rode your bike over that cliff, it was Him who lifted you and carried you across as His plans for you had not yet been fulfilled."

He said some other stuff but, to tell you the truth, I didn't hear anything else. I was overwhelmed with what I had just heard. My wife heard it, and thankfully, I had shared the story of my bike accident with her although I had never told anyone else about it. I stood in tears and awe that the Lord would so clearly and distinctly speak to me. There was no denying it — I couldn't explain it away.

I never saw that man again, but I have never forgotten the night that the Lord confirmed His call on my life. He put a dream in my heart that I have never gotten over. It is that word that drives me when I get discouraged. When nothing seems to make any sense in my life, I thank the Lord for speaking so clearly to me that I will never forget it.

There was another time the Lord spoke to my heart to confirm a purpose or destiny. This time was only recently. My wife and I were in Chicago, and I was awakened during the night by a voice. I was extremely startled as it seemed as though someone was in the room. I then realized that my Heavenly Father had spoken a fresh word into my spirit so loudly, I could never deny it. It renewed my faith that what the Lord had started in me, He would perfect. He had chosen to awaken me in the middle of the night, and there was no denying it was the voice of the Lord. I quickly recorded it in my journal so that I would never forget that moment. I wanted to make sure that whenever the word was proven true in my life, I would have a record of that night to renew my faith once again and encourage my destiny.

Perhaps you have never had an experience as strange as what I have described for you. I only share my story to encourage your faith that God has a purpose for you. When you want to give up, remember the Word of the Lord to you, His plan, and His purpose — a God-sized destiny that only He can fulfill.

Perhaps you say, "I am a nobody with little to offer." Then praise the Lord, you are a perfect candidate for God to use to feed a famine-struck society! Thankfully, He is not a respecter of persons. He can and does put His fire on some of the most unlikely candidates according to the world's standards.

Joseph was just a young man when God put purpose in his life through a vision. I believe, more often than not, purpose finds you instead of you finding purpose. Purpose comes as a result of vision. I think it is important to note that the road from vision to purpose to activity is a journey.

Vision drives the purpose; purpose drives the passion; and passion drives the activity. A lot has been written on vision — what it is and what it is not. Without over-simplifying it and without discrediting many great books written on the topic of vision, let me state it simply: vision is getting pregnant — period. That's it! I know you think I have lost my mind. Let me explain.

No one is ever neutral on pregnancy. They are either very excited about it or very sad because of it. The ones who are happy are the ones who wanted to be pregnant. Here is the question for you today: are you pregnant with some vision, hope, or promise that produces incredible joy of coming life?

In the physical sense, we call it expecting — expecting what? It means expecting or believing that something is on its way. In the spiritual sense, sadly most Christians aren't pregnant — they aren't expecting anything except to hopefully go to Heaven someday.

What a tragedy! Here is what I mean: I look forward to Heaven, but I want abundant life now also. I want to walk in the power of the Holy Spirit and make a difference today! Getting saved for the purpose of *only* going to Heaven is not embracing the total work of Jesus on the cross. It is a very shallow motivation.

Isaiah 54 states that our husband is also our maker; therefore, we should stay pregnant and always be in an expecting mode. Peter Lord, Pastor of First Baptist Church in Titusville Florida, preached a message once as only Peter can called, "God Won't Move In With You until You Marry Him." His point was that we can't get pregnant spiritually until we marry God or make a covenant with him — the same thing a marriage contract is. It's a covenant. Then, out of love and intimacy with and for God, we get pregnant with the life of God.

Does your life reveal that you're pregnant? Do the activities of your life reveal the expectation of coming life? When my wife, Debbie, became pregnant with our first child, our life changed drastically even before he was born. We started shopping a lot. We were buying nursery items, stocking up on baby clothes, painting the nursery — getting ready. We also talked a lot about it. If you want to know if someone is spiritually pregnant, just listen to what they say or probably more importantly, what they don't say.

When we get pregnant by the Spirit of God, we talk a lot about that also. Our conversations reveal the expectancy of life as do our activities. Our conversations are full of hope, life, and joy.

Contrastingly, you can get pregnant by the devil. Whoever you are intimate with is who you will get pregnant by. This pregnancy is death — no hope, no promise, no joy of expecting life, just death. Do you know people like this? Sure you do. We all do.

Each of us chooses the level of intimacy we want with God. Listen carefully; you are as close to God as you want to be. Many people blame their lack of intimacy with God on a shortage of time, bad genes, fatigue, demands of children, and the list goes on. The fact is we really need to evaluate how important intimacy with God is to us.

If the doctor told you that you needed heart surgery or you were going to die within the month, you would not say, "Oh well, I will get around to it someday when I am not so busy." It would become your top priority! We must view intimacy with God the same way.

God led his people out of bondage and provided everything they needed, yet they chose to stay at the bottom of Mount Sinai. Paraphrased, they said, "Moses, you go on up there with God. We will stay down here, and then you can come back and tell us what God said. That's as close to God as we want to be. In fact, God looks like a consuming fire up there." Please notice that to Moses, the fire was a purifying fire. He got face to face with God. The scripture says he talked with God face to face as one friend talks with another.

Only the people who were standing a long way from the presence of God saw the fire of God as scary and preferred to keep their distance. People are still the same today — they stand at a distance choosing to let someone else always hear God and tell them what He said. They never hear God for themselves. When you stand at a distance, all you can see is a consuming fire. Desire for intimacy with God, will allow you to stand in the fire knowing that it is a purifying fire that draws you ever closer and closer to God himself.

When we choose to stand at distance from God, and He doesn't meet our needs or expectations, we tend to form a new god out of whatever is valuable to us at the time. This is what the Hebrews did, and we still do it today. We take the valuable things that God himself has given us, make them our god, and worship an image we created. We will worship *the God* or we will make *a god* for ourselves. To what or to who is your knee bowed today?

When God gave Joseph the vision of his destiny — got him pregnant — he did not understand it and he did not do anything to fulfill it. He just lived his life with awareness and expectation. When things came along that seemed bad and very trying, the expectancy Joseph had in his heart allowed him to move through the trial. It doesn't mean it was without pain; it just means there was always hope. In fact, the birth process is one of contractions and pain that forces the life to become evident.

Unfortunately, abortion is an option. If the pain and inconvenience of a coming life is a cramp in our selfish lifestyle, we can get rid of it. Many Christians want to be on some form of spiritual birth control. They only want to be pregnant when they get good and ready and when it in no way disrupts their "me-first" mentality they have. One product of vision is always hope — hope that will allow you to move through the worst of circumstances. Hebrews 12:2 says, "… Who for the joy (hope) set before him, He endured the cross …" It was the hope of His destiny and the hope of His vision that allowed Jesus to endure the cross.

The reason it may have taken me so long to realize my destiny is that I took some detours along the way that made the journey longer than it had to be. God's people did the same thing in the wilderness. Moses did it trying to fulfill his destiny in his own way and his own power. I once heard that an armadillo can put a pregnancy on hold until more favorable conditions exist. The Hebrew people put pregnancy on hold for 40 years!

While God's plan for you was written before the creation, it is not written on your heart by the Spirit until you give your life to Christ. In Christ, it moves from *outside* the heart to *inside* the heart. People who do not know Christ also have destiny, but it is written in their minds. It doesn't produce lasting hope. It's not empowered by the supernatural power of God. It may produce activity and a measure of success, but it is "Christ in you, the hope of glory."

I want hope that is bigger than I am! I want hope that allows me to cooperate with the Holy Spirit. Moses went from being a man of strength and power to being a shepherd before God used him in a mighty way to deliver His people. Do you see how he descended into greatness?

The communication of your destiny to others should be a cautious thing. Joseph told his family that they would someday bow before him. That did not settle well with all those around him. However, everything that happened to him afterward pushed him toward his destiny. He had to grow into his destiny while his destiny grew within him.

Right now, you are probably confirming the destiny in your heart or you are questioning your destiny. So many people say, "I do not know what my purpose here on earth is." I wonder if those people really want to know or would they prefer to just roam aimlessly through life and blame everyone and everything for their hopelessness.

If you have invited Christ into your life, then ask Him to reveal your purpose. Scripture tells us that we have the ability to hear the voice of our Heavenly Father. Trust that voice — He does have a purpose for you. Start asking God to show you the detours you have taken that have slowed down His purpose in you. Then, repent and follow God. Repentance will immediately put you back on the right path. It may still take a little while to get back on the right road, but at least you will be going in the right direction.

When the prodigal son finally came to his senses — that means he got as miserable, lonely, and unfulfilled as he could be — he acknowledged that he had taken a long detour, got up, and started walking towards his Father. One step at a time, he walked. Along the way, while humbled, he assumed he had forfeited his destiny and he was going to have to settle for second (lower) status in the family. Man, was he surprised when he got home! Even though he had a long and convincing speech planned, the first thing his father did was reaffirm his destiny — his sonship. He was a son before he left, he was a son while he was away, and he was a son upon his return. While he was gone, he sacrificed the benefits of sonship but not the bloodline or the destiny.

I would be remiss to not point out here that his older brother was also doing the same thing — it just looked more religious. His brother was standing outside the house complaining about not having a destiny. His father went out to him and also reminded him of his destiny. However, he refused to come to the party. Many Christians are standing outside claiming to be religious and are missing the party inside with the Father. Worse than that, they are pointing the finger at others and judging as unworthy those who came home, embraced their destiny, and entered the party.

Where are you today? Have you walked away from your destiny and found yourself in a place you can't stand? If so, get up and go home. Your destiny awaits you. Are you at home but standing outside angry? Do you feel like you have done all the right stuff and the party has passed you by? If this is you, drop the judgementalism and get inside the house. There is a party going on! Inside, in the presence of your Father, destiny still awaits you. Have you ever been born again? If not, invite Christ into your heart right now and hear him invite you to the party. Go on inside, your destiny awaits you! Vision will allow Genesis 50:20 to get into your heart and create an awareness of something bigger than you: "And as for you, you meant evil against me, but God meant it for good in order to bring about this present result, to preserve many people alive."

As we walk through the remaining steps of this process of descending into greatness, remember that it all begins with a dream, a vision, and a destiny! It requires the ability to see with your heart what your eyes cannot see and the willingness to follow God when you don't understand. Walk with me now as we continue down to the top.

2 Living Past the Pain of Rejection

No one ever fulfills his or her destiny without experiencing rejection along the way. Many times, similar to Joseph, we are full of enthusiasm about our purpose only to find out others are not. In fact, not only are they not excited about our vision, they are actually opposed to it and seem to be on a mission to quench our dream.

Joseph's father rebuked the dream, and his brothers hated the dreamer. Often those closest to us seem the least interested and seem to resist us — to oppose us! We ask ourselves "Why?" over and over again. While the answer is clear, it is still a painful process — very painful. You see, the resistance makes us more focused and more God-dependent. It is also interesting that God uses Joseph's brothers the most to ensure the dream is fulfilled. It's strange how God works that way, isn't it?

When people mock, scorn, and resist you, stay strong because God will use them to accomplish his purpose in you life and fulfill the dream. I have found that the people who oppose us the most are usually people with no dream of their own. People who don't hear God don't want someone else to hear him either. Rather than admit they have a hearing problem, they just condemn and make fun of you.

The dreamless are usually the meanest. There are a few exceptions; but most of us want to jump off a bridge many times along the journey. It's a frustrating process — you don't know your purpose, then you do know it, people seem to hate you for it, and then you give up only to find it there again. Pretty crazy, huh?

God designs us to be rejected by men. Why? Because ultimately our only acceptance can be found in Him. As long as our acceptance is in anything other than Christ, we cannot be trusted in a Joseph position because He knows that we would allow the rejection of man to cause us to mishandle God's treasure — His children.

Rejection is a very painful thing, and many people throughout this world suffer great pain as a result of rejection. We all know people who are mad at the world and trust no one because they were rejected. When we were in elementary school, how much damage was done to people who were not chosen to be on a team until no one else was left? I can remember the look of several of my schoolmates even today. They stood there day after day after day and waited until everyone else was picked and then heard someone say, "Well, I guess we have to take John," or "I guess we are stuck with Tommy." While we learn the pain of rejection early, we also learn the tremendous fulfillment of acceptance. Acceptance becomes our god or idol, and we live our life for acceptance.

Please don't speed by that thought too quickly. Acceptance can be and is a major idol that our society worships. God made it very clear from the beginning that there should not be any other gods before Him. Acceptance will cause you to say and do things outside the will of God in order to gain the acceptance others. We become people pleasers. We say the right things around the right people to make sure we are noticed, appreciated, and accepted. We reserve the words "thank you" for those who will notice and appreciate us more for it. At the same time, it is withheld from those we deem meaningless.

We manage our behavior when necessary in order to be noticed. Jesus was quick to tell his disciples that they should not be like the Pharisees who only did things to be seen and noticed. He called them "white-washed tombs." Jesus said that they had received their reward in full. In other words, the only reward they would get is the one they got — the atta-boys from people.

The idol or god of acceptance does not work alone. When we worship the god of acceptance, manipulation and intimidation will become the traits of our life. That's because everything is about us — I will do and say anything to anyone because life is about me and what I want and need. While it hides itself in various forms, at the root is the demand for acceptance — I will either do the things necessary for the people I deem important to accept me, or I will, through manipulation and intimidation, force you to accept me. Either way, it's all about me.

We will never descend to the top unless we tear down the idol of acceptance. Tearing it down begins with admitting this is where we are and who we have become. You might be one of those people who say, "I don't care what anybody thinks, they can take me as I am or not at all!" What you're saying is that you are demanding to be accepted — I will only accept you IF you accept me. Acceptance is your god and your life will be controlled by it.

Even Jesus stated that His Father's will was more important than His own was. Christ — the perfect man; the lover of mankind — was rejected. If He was rejected, what makes us think we will not be? In Matthew 11:27, Jesus said, "No one knows the Son except the Father, and no one knows the Father except the Son and anyone to whom the Son desires to reveal Him."

Joseph was left at home while his brothers went off to tend the flocks. When he got the nod from his father to go and check on them, little did he realize that he was headed for rejection. He located them only to find he is the object of their hatred — despised and rejected. They are so mad about this punk kid's vision and his father's favor that they were willing to do anything to punish him — yes, even kill him.

Isn't it amazing what our minds will convince our hearts to do? The reason they are so furious is that they are experiencing rejection. It's not real rejection, mind you; it's perceived rejection. The enemy will fill our minds with "poor me, pity me, pamper me, feel sorry for me, no one loves me" language until we are in a wilderness of isolation and contempt for life and everyone in it.

They were convinced that their father had rejected them by accepting and giving preference to their kid brother. They thought it was outrageous to be told that they would bow down to him! That is rejection by God Himself! They thought, "Let's throw him into a pit and let an animal eat him. Then, we'll claim innocence, and rid ourselves of this rejection we feel."

Rejection, however, is neither a person nor a group of people. It is a spirit straight from hell. You could eliminate everyone in your life, and you would not eliminate the feeling of rejection. You can surround yourself with people who you think accept you, and yet always question who they really are and what they really think.

I am convinced that many people are tormented daily and look for the next person they can destroy or remove from their path because of a deep-seated feeling of rejection. It is a stronghold of the enemy deep within their spirit that consumes their life, their thoughts, and ultimately their actions. They are always plotting in order to assure their acceptance.

If we make acceptance our god, we will worship it. It will become our idol of choice. Our actions and activities will always focus on ensuring our acceptance. We will trade the favor of God for the favor of man and leave emotional corpses everywhere we go. Unforgiveness and bitterness will consume us.

Christ, while experiencing the ultimate rejection, said, "My God, My God, why have you forsaken me?" He quickly added, "Into your hands, I commit my soul" (Luke 23:46). Christ understood and embraced His destiny so well that He was able to say, "Father, forgive them, they do not know what they are doing" (Luke 32:34). He said this while looking at the very people who rejected Him and condemned Him to death on a cross.

If we are to become great godly leaders, we must repent of worshipping acceptance and acknowledge that we have created an idol in our own image. Rejection will continually confront us because the enemy wants to discredit us by influencing us to focus on ourselves.

We must remember that Satan is still very angry that his attempt to make himself accepted and honored was defeated. He wanted to establish his kingdom and be the "big kahuna" — number one, greatest of all the angels! His focus was on himself. We will never reflect the glory of the Lord while staring at ourselves. We must look at Him, lay down our kingdom, and declare, "No matter what rejection comes, Father, I choose your kingdom over my own. I repent of worshipping the acceptance of man. I choose to embrace the acceptance of the God who created me and put destiny in my heart."

3 What's Seducing You?

In the life of Joseph, seduction was in the sexual form. At least that is all the Bible chooses to describe. However, while this is and can be a huge form of seduction, there are many other forms also. In Genesis 39:7-9, we find Joseph as the object of focus of his boss' wife. She wants him and she wants him bad. Day after day, she stares at this hunk and thinks, "What if?"

She is probably turned on even more because he is a man of integrity. He doesn't flirt, he doesn't try to catch her eye, he just faithfully serves his master. People are so captivated by integrity that they will sometimes do anything to be near it. At the same time, the enemy is assaulting our integrity and our character in order to ruin our reputation and our credibility.

There are many things that can seduce us and cause us to compromise *who* and *whose* we are.

We can be seduced by power, prestige, the applause of men, fame, wealth — you name it and the enemy will try to use it for his glory.

Another word for seduction can be temptation. Temptation is the process whereby our lust and desires are exposed. God put desires in us and a godly means of meeting those needs. God then permits the enemy to tempt us in order to reveal to us the areas where we have not trusted Him.

What are you being tempted by? If you are in a time of wilderness in your life, look out! That is when the enemy is the loudest. Sometimes we are led of the Spirit into the wilderness.

"And Jesus, full of the Holy Spirit, returned from the Jordan and was led about by the Spirit in the wilderness."

Luke 4:1

God, because of His love for us, wants to expose our weaknesses so that we might depend upon Him for strength. When Satan tempted Jesus for 40 days, Jesus just declared what God said — that He was who His Father said He was, that He could do what His Father said He could do, and that His Father would provide everything He needed. Luke 4:13 says, "And when the devil had finished every temptation, he departed from Him until a more opportune time."

Just because you stand firm today does not mean that the devil has finished seducing you. What is seducing you away from godliness? What is seducing you away from your God-given dreams? Acknowledge it and flee from it.

Samson, a great and powerful man on a mission from God almighty, was seduced away. The story in Judges 13 portrays Samson as a man who was called, appointed, and anointed by God. He was a spiritual Rambo — a man of great power! However, Sam had a big weakness. He thought he was indestructible! Because of the evidence of God in his life, he thought he could play with the world and be unaffected.

Never be fooled into thinking that just because you are a man or woman of God with evidence of God's favor in your life that you are indestructible! Just because you say "no" once to whatever is seducing you away, it does not mean you are free forever. It does not mean you can do anything without adverse consequences. Never confuse the patience of God with powerlessness or apathy.

Isn't it sad that Samson is known as much or more for his Delilah as he was for himself? It is hard to think of Samson without the word Delilah popping up — Samson and Delilah. We have heard the same names used over and over again from childhood Sunday school to Christian storybooks.

What is your Delilah? We all have one. It is whatever entices or seduces us away from God's call — His mission and purpose for our life. It is whatever would cause you to sacrifice your God-given power and strength. The enemy knows which buttons to push to render us ineffective in God's plan and purpose for us. He wants to bring us to that place of compromise so that he can rob us of our strength at our weakest moment!

This did not happen to Samson all at once and it will probably not happen to you all at once either. Samson began to play with his strength. He no longer protected and cherished the gifts that God had bestowed upon him. He took it for granted and let the enemy use it as a toy. "I can do this without it affecting me. I am indestructible. I am Samson!" he might have thought.

Do you find yourself thinking the same thing? Do you find yourself playing with and not respecting or protecting what God has entrusted to you? Has there been a time when the truth has been more important to you than it is at this particular time in your life? Have you ever found yourself making peace with occasionally inflating your expense reports? Have you ever decided that it is okay to occasionally hurt or de-value people with whom you associate? Is it really innocent fun to catch the eye of someone at work? It's just a little flirting — it's harmless, right? WRONG! You are playing with the enemy and thinking you are indestructible.

Samson played the game also until one day he compromised his God-given strength by allowing Delilah to touch his hair — the source of his strength. She wanted to render him helpless. She nagged him day and night until he revealed that she could render him weak if she wove the locks of his hair. Please see the progression. He allowed her to touch his hair because she was nagging him to death!

Genesis 16:19 says, "And she made him sleep on her knees and called for a man and had him shave off the seven locks of his hair. Then she began to afflict him and his strength left him." Just like Delilah, the enemy is persistent and will stop at nothing to exploit our weaknesses and render us weak and ineffective.

Don't you see the depth to which he sank without realizing it? He was so at peace that he fell asleep in the lap of the enemy. There was no fear or cause for alarm. He was just lying there letting the enemy destroy him!

As soon as the source of his strength was gone, affliction came and he was powerless. Genesis 16:20 continues: "And she said, 'The Philistines are upon you, Samson!' And he awoke from his sleep and said, 'I will go out as at other times and shake myself free.' But he did not know that the Lord had departed from him."

This is the horrible reality. Many people are walking around today thinking they still have their God-given strength, and they do not know the condition of their weakness. Samson thought he still had his strength. The result of losing our strength is more serious than we might immediately perceive. Let me take a moment to point out how serious and detrimental this is.

Nehemiah 8:10 says, "The joy of the Lord is my strength." When we compromise our strength and play with our power, we lose our joy. Sleep becomes difficult. There seems to be no purpose in our life anymore.

How many joyless Christians do you know who just live in a daze? They seem to have no life or sense of purpose. With most, it is possible to point to a time when, through seduction, they lost their strength and subsequently lost their joy. Some have been seduced out of one church after another, one marriage after another, and the list goes on.

When Peter heard the third crow of the cock, he realized he had lost his joy. His strength was gone. Where did the Peter go who screamed he would die for his Lord? He walked, full of guilt and shame, back to the only the thing he knew — fishing. Thank God that we serve a God who is into restoration and whose mercy is everlasting! That means it won't run out.

You may say, "I've used up a lot of God's mercy," but He hasn't noticed! He does not snuff out a smoldering candle. Instead, He relights it. He will not throw away a bruised reed; He restores it as a useable instrument. He can put his fire on any old bush and any old bush will do! That includes you!

I know this kind of talk makes legalists mad. Right now, many are furious that I would insinuate that God gives grace and mercy to people who do not deserve it. Some well-meaning people think that they are holy enough on their own merit to have God's favor. Unfortunately, they are like the older brother who is standing outside the house mad at his father for throwing a party for someone who does not deserve it. He is the one who deserves it, he thinks. Right now, that person needs to repent as well and stop playing with the patience of God. We have all sinned and fallen short of the glory of God. You can do all the right stuff and be joyless, too.

Second, we lose our vision. The enemy took Samson's eyes and made him blind. Oh, the pain of losing your vision. Imagine not being able to see the hand of the Lord in what you do and who you are. Imagine having to be led everywhere with no sense of direction — roaming aimlessly. The Bible says that without vision, the people perish. How true that is.

Third, we lose our freedom. Samson became a captive. Others dictated his activity and his actions. Everything he had belonged to someone else. He became a prisoner.

Fourth, our labor becomes very difficult. Samson did the work of an animal. It was hard and boring as he pushed the grinding wheel day in and day out. His muscles ached. Sweat filled his useless eyes, and they burned with irritation. While he may have lost his incredible power, he was still no weakling. I think we assume that with the loss of his hair, all of his strength left him. Not quite! It took quite a man to replace the strength of an ox. What he lost was his supernatural, God-empowered strength, and his God-empowered purpose. He lost his joy.

Lastly, we become prey for the world to mock. Can you imagine the sound of the crowd as they mocked him? "Hey Samson, what are you going to do today, old powerful one?" They laughed as they watched this once-powerful man go round and round and round and round with no joy, freedom, vision, or strength. Weakness and powerlessness were his attributes. Samson became the entertainment of the city. They would call him to amuse themselves.

However, Judges 16:21 is followed by Judges 16:22! The verse starts with "However" — thank the Lord Almighty that our God is a God of *howevers!* "However, the hair of his head began to grow again after it was shaved off." Nothing is final until God says it is final. His hair began to grow again, and he asked his Lord to once again strengthen him, and the Lord said, "Yes." How merciful He is.

Your Delilah could be your friends, career, uncontrolled emotions, past hurts, bitterness, unforgiveness, or immorality just to name a few possibilities. This question will help you identify your Delilah — what is it that is always nagging you? Answer that question and you identify the source of your seduction.

Have you reached the point where you would do anything to have your strength back? Samson was willing to give up his life to once again experience the presence and the power of God. We say, "Lord, I will do anything. I just want your anointing back. I want the joy back. I want you, Lord." Are you there right now?"

Unfortunately, many of us have walked this path. We know how lonely and joyless this can be. If you are at that place in your life, repent and watch as your hair begins to grow again. He is not done with you. It may be different than it could have been, but He has not forsaken you. Romans 11:29 says, "The gifts and callings of the Lord are irrevocable."

Many leaders fall at this point and never make an impact again. This test will expose our weaknesses if we let it; it will show God's mercy and strength if we allow it. No leader can be in a position to feed a famine-struck society unless he has recognized and dealt with his Delilah.

4 False Accusation Always Hurts

Everyone who has ever assumed a position of leadership knows the pain of being falsely accused. In fact, anyone who has lived on this planet has experienced that pain. Consider what I am about to say carefully. This test will cause you to destroy yourself emotionally, professionally, and spiritually if you assume the full responsibility for your own vindication. You may say, "Sure, but it's destroying my reputation." Stay faithful to God and He will vindicate you. You cannot vindicate yourself. If you try to handle it alone, you will open yourself up to a bigger set of problems.

Joseph, while doing all the right things and fleeing the seduction found himself falsely accused. How could he have avoided it? I'm not sure he could have. When people want to destroy you, there is nothing you can do to stop them. Of course, he probably could have avoided some of the problems by not allowing himself to be in a room with her alone. Didn't he notice her glances? That should have been a red flag. He pushed her away but in the end, he became the target of an angry, rejected woman. Revenge was hers — or so she thought.

Joseph paid the price for the accusation. He was imprisoned for a crime he did not commit. However, the scripture says in Genesis 39:21, "But the Lord was with Joseph and extended kindness to him and gave him favor in the sight of the chief jailer."

Anytime you find yourself falsely accused, you must remember that the Lord is with you. His kindness will sustain you and his favor will once again exalt you.

Soon, the chief jailer put Joseph in charge of the jail. Yes, Joseph was in the prison as a prisoner, but the Lord was with him. The Lord gave him favor, and He used the time to continue to perfect Joseph's leadership qualities. Then in Genesis 39:23, the Bible tells us, "… and whatever he did, the Lord made to prosper." Just because the world forsakes you, it never ever means the Lord will forsake you. He will complete the work he started in you! As long as we are faithful to serve where we are, give God the glory, and trust in His vindication, we will come out refined and more Christ-like than we would or could have been otherwise.

When Bill Clinton was accused of sexual immorality, we all watched him tell the country that he did not do it — he told us point blank, in our face, "I did not do it." When you are confronted with something you did do, admit it, learn from it, and make sure you don't do it again. When you are falsely accused, continue to serve, love, bless, forgive, and glorify. Jesus was falsely accused. He could have stopped it all, but he did nothing. Then, on the cross, He was vindicated by his Father. All the while, interceding in our behalf, he said, "Father, forgive them, for they know not what they do."

Whatever you do, throughout all tests, walk in continuous forgiveness. If you don't, bitterness will flood your soul and revenge will fill your heart. There will be destroyed, abused, and damaged people in your wake. If you are innocent, God will vindicate you — I promise. It may not be when or how you want but you will be vindicated.

False accusation brings us to the place where we have to either trust or open the door of our mind for a new stronghold. If we don't trust God, we ultimately grieve the Holy Spirit.

Ephesians 4:30-32 says, "And do not grieve the Holy Spirit of God, by whom you were sealed for the day of redemption. Let all bitterness and wrath and anger and clamor and slander be put away from you, along with all malice. And be kind to one another, tender-hearted, forgiving each other, just as God in Christ also has forgiven you."

Pikria — Greek for bitterness — is not only the opposite of sweetness but also of kindness. *Spite* harbors resentment and keeps a score of wrongs. Aristotle defined those who display it as "hard to be reconciled." *Rage* is what flows from bitterness in an outburst of uncontrolled passion and frustration. *Anger* here signifies an unjustifiable human emotion that manifests itself in noisy assertiveness, shouting, brawling, and abuse.

Yes, trying to vindicate ourselves will lead us down a path of heartache, frustration, and bitterness. Stay faithful, serving, and kind-hearted. God will vindicate you.

5 Detouring Past Disappointment

Disappointment comes when we think God is no longer in control or God is no longer meeting our expectations. As we live in expectation and anticipation of our dreams, we will face dashed hopes, defeated plans, and overlooked effort. Our expectations must be on Him and Him alone. We shouldn't spend the rest of our lives moaning and walking around with our tails between our legs. God is in control.

As simple as it sounds, either we trust Him or we don't. Jesus once said, "I assure you: Whoever does not welcome the kingdom of God like a little child will never enter it" (Mark 10:15, Holman Christian Standard Bible). He was saying we should come to Him in trust as a child comes to a parent.

Being a dreamer has the ability to produce a lot of uncertainty. We are always looking out there

— dreaming, wondering, planning, and expecting. We think everyone should be as excited about what we see as we are.

Unfortunately — or fortunately — that is not the case. Sometimes the Lord allows us to dream big dreams in order to help us hold on to the hope. While we persevere under trial, we are sifted and refined. Other times, he puts the destiny in our hearts so that when He says, "Now," we know which direction to run. You can count on a dreamer to always be sitting ready to run somewhere. We have a million miles to cover, a short period to get there, and another destination waiting after that one. It's our nature.

My wife, bless her heart, has had to live with that for now over 27 years. She is Mrs. Methodical, Mrs. Practical, Mrs. Structure, and she sometimes thinks she is married to an absolute mad man. She cringes every time I walk into the room with "the look." She knows it well. It's the dreamer look that says, "I just wanted to let you know I am changing jobs," or "We are moving to Hong Kong," or "I have decided to write a book on the life of a dreamer." She just hangs on and tries to temper my enthusiasm with some sort of sanity.

All of us who are of the dreamer type had better thank God above he put a sensible mate in our life. He knew what we needed because He created us that way. He knew what we would become. I also try to surround myself with a few of the more stable types in my business also. More than once, these valued partners have slowed me down enough to prevent a major wreck.

With all that zeal and enthusiasm comes disappointment and dashed hopes. We have to remember, once again, not to get mad or develop an unforgiving spirit. We have to understand that we shouldn't hold the world and everybody in it responsible for things not happening when and how we want. God is in control and we can trust him. Better yet, He will use these times to clarify the vision, fine-tune our purpose, and properly connect us to others.

Joseph found favor in that prison and became the leader of it. When a couple of Pharaoh's staff were thrown into jail for making their king mad, Joseph was put in charge of them and took good care of them. One night, they each had a dream and were very perplexed about what it meant. Joseph interpreted it for them and asked the cupbearer to remember him when was reinstated into Pharaoh's service. The cupbearer assured him that he would.

However, Genesis 40:23 says, "Yet the chief cupbearer did not remember Joseph, but forgot him." It was two more years before Joseph had an opportunity to get out of that prison. He just kept serving people even though he had unrewarded labor and dashed hopes.

We have all experienced the pain of working hard — to accomplish something at work or church or maybe when we achieved some personal goal — and no one even seemed to notice. We serve and serve. While we don't do it for the recognition, sometimes it is encouraging to know that our service has a great enough impact that someone might notice. At least it would confirm that we're not wasting our time.

Joseph modeled the greatness of serving when no one was looking or noticing. He adopted an attitude and lifestyle of "I will continue to serve even if no one ever notices." Someone once said, "It's amazing how much we can get done when we don't care who gets the credit." How true it is.

Success: The Greatest Test of All

"Nearly all men can stand adversity, but if you want to test a man's character, give him power."

Abraham Lincoln (1809-1865)

You could easily assume that once you successfully complete the other entire test necessary for you to realize your dream that you would automatically be ready. However, this test may be the greatest one of all. What type of person will you be when the power and authority are yours? When you realize your dream, how will you treat those who rejected you? What will you do with the people who falsely accused you? How will you respond to the people who held up your dreams and caused the pain of your disappointment? Will you love or destroy those people who dashed your dreams? Will your attitude be, "Look out! What goes around comes around, buddy"? Let's look at how Joseph responded as he modeled the grace and love of God.

First, Joseph just continued to serve and remain a man under authority. Here is where the test reveals our character. Will we use the opportunity of being in authority to be out from under authority? Joseph remained willingly under the authority of Pharaoh and his God.

If we don't walk through and descend into authority, we often find ourselves wanting to be free of authority. We want to be "the man." We desire to be recognized, respected, and rewarded. After all, we have paid a great price to be here.

Authority has always been a big issue. It was the original struggle of the universe. Satan wanted authority, position, power, and prestige, but he did not want to be under authority.

The thing that made Joseph a great godly leader was his heart to be under authority. In his father's house, he was a man under authority; in Potiphar's house, he was a man under authority; in the prison, he was a man under authority; and in Pharaoh's kingdom, he was a man under authority.

Submission to authority is not so much an action as it is a condition of the heart — it is an attribute of the heart and the epitome of character. For many leaders, the move upward is a "me-first" mentality. It causes people to walk over anyone in their way in their quest for authority.

Jesus was the perfect example of a man under authority. Picture Jesus at the final supper with his disciples. He poured his life into these men. He had walked with them, modeled godliness for them, encouraged them, and corrected them — oh, how He loved them. They entered the room and, even at this hour, they were thinking of themselves, "Who will be the greatest in the kingdom? Who will sit on the right and on the left?" The room was full of me-centeredness, "What about me! What about me? Notice me! Look at me. Reward me. ME, ME, ME!" Jesus, the one who was about to walk to the hill and die for them, modeled servanthood one more time. He didn't scream, "Well, if no else is going to wash feet, I will!"

Instead, He quietly walked over to the basin, put on the clothes of the lowest servant, picked up the water jar and the basin, and did again what He had done since his arrival on earth — He showed us the necessity of being a servant above all else. Without hesitation, he took off his priestly garment and put on a servant's garment. He walked over to the first disciple, knelt in front of him, and removed his sandals. With love in his eyes and the gentleness of his hands, he washed the feet of the first disciple. I suspect no one noticed for a while. While the room buzzed with, "What about me," Jesus was on his knees serving.

He gently removed the sandals of Judas. His eyes filled with tears as he washed the feet of the disciple who in only a short while would sell him out. Jesus' heart was broken because he loved Judas so much. He loved all His disciples. No matter what they did or were about to do, He still loved and served them. I can imagine a hush quickly fell over the room as they noticed that Jesus was, without prompting or recognition, serving mankind in the lowliest form.

Any person who has descended into greatness doesn't wait around expecting someone to serve them. They are always looking for an opportunity to serve. No task is too good for them. No task is too small or menial. No relationship is too insignificant. They don't have to call attention to themselves. No one has to notice and acknowledge. It's just who they are. They serve wherever God puts them as unto Him. They even love the unlovable.

I am often saddened by how some Christians will only love and serve those whom they deem deserving. We are never more un-Christ-like than when we turn our backs on God's kids because they don't deserve our love. We can turn the most trivial things into an issue — "We brought colored toothpicks to a dinner at their house and the hostess did not even say 'thank you.' We loved them and she didn't act like they meant anything to her." Whatever the reason, refusal to love or refusal to serve is the equivalent of not following the example of our Lord.

Ask yourself right now, whose feet would you be unwilling to wash? Would you, with a broken heart full of love, have washed the feet of your betrayer? If right now, you can think of someone whose feet you would not wash, you have not descended enough to be mightily used of God. We all know people who serve continuously who want to be noticed for it. These are the ones who, if they don't get the recognition they think they deserve, quit serving, leave the church, resent the world, abandon a relationship, walk away from a friendship, talk about everyone, and blame everyone for their misery. This is not the heart of a godly servant. Jesus did not come into the world *to be served* but *to serve* and give His life as a ransom for many.

Ultimately, success should look like this: a humble servant who values people over position or power and individuals over institutions. It should be someone who loves unconditionally and serves even those who do not deserve it unto His glory. If today you are withholding love and acceptance, repent and receive the mercy of a loving Father who thankfully has never withheld anything from you. I assure you times of refreshing will come.

7 Jesus: Our Perfect Example

"He that falls in love with himself will have no rivals."

Ben Franklin (1706-1790)

God does not have a problem with His children being in places of honor. In reality, He longs to exalt us. What concerns Him is upward mobility as defined by the world — to advance our own cause, push our own agenda, or build our own kingdom. A call to downward mobility does not paint a picture of men and women drained and empty, devoid of personality and energy. Downward mobility — descending into greatness — means that we allow God to determine what needs are legitimate. It means yielding our desires and passions to His guidance. It means that we use our gifts and talents without applause or recognition. It means that we will conform our dreams to His will.

Upward mobility as a strategy to success will produce a social hierarchy or "pecking order." Pecking order is based upon the natural process of dominance in a group of social animals such as chickens. For instance, put 10 chickens in a pen together and spread a little feed. You will soon witness an amazing phenomenon. In a matter of minutes, they will instinctively determine through a series of skirmishes who the number one chicken will be, the number two chicken, and so on finally leaving a chicken as the number ten chicken. Chicken number one pecks at and intimidates chicken number two; chicken number two pecks at and intimidates chicken number three, etc.

In my younger adult life, we had horses and we saw them do the same thing. Put 20 horses in a pasture together and come back the next day. There will be scars of war everywhere and the new king horse will be identified and greatly feared. You just have to watch them a short while to see how they identify the pecking order.

We once had a wonderful mare named Wendy. She was about 13 years old, not very tall, and only weighed about 900 pounds. She was the gentlest horse I have ever been around. She loved people and loved being touched and pampered. My children treated her like a big dog. They would actually lay down with her. On more than one occasion, I have walked into the stable to find Wendy laying down asleep with my son laying beside her or partially on her. She was so meek and gentle that she was also the final horse in any pecking order. We would have to feed her by herself, away from the other horses, or she would never get to eat. The other horses would run her away from her own food.

Sadly, this same kind of thing happens everywhere. At parties, class reunions, church, work, and most everywhere, there are people. No one is immune to this sickness. We look at other people's homes, wardrobes, cars, education, business, and influence, and we try to figure out where they fit in the pecking order. It may seem harmless but there is something involved here that runs deep in every human heart, and there is nothing innocent about it. It's serious and dangerous because it radically affects how we relate to one another.

Our tendency is to treat those above us with admiration, respect, and honor even if we despise them. We then treat those below us with insensitivity, callousness, or even contempt. The deception is that it does resemble order in a world filled with chaos. There is comfort in knowing where we fit. To know when and to whom to peck or be pecked by brings a sick, distorted acceptance that we have made peace with. We love labels — white collar, blue collar, management, labor, Baptist, Methodist, charismatic, non-charismatic — and the list goes on.

In all of history, no one was more qualified for the pecking order than Jesus was. Think about it. He owned everything and He created everybody. He could have chosen any profession and been the major player of any company or political circle. It was His for the taking!

The problem was that He hated the pecking order. In fact, He spent most of His ministry ripping at its foundations. With His words, He scorned those who had reached the top such as the Pharisees and religious leaders. He called them snakes, hypocrites, and "white-washed tombs." He accused them of robbing widows, being filled with dead men's bones, and worshipping themselves.

Their problem was one of focus. They focused on the externals or how they appeared on the outside. That's why they loved the Neiman Marcus robes, demanded the best season ticket seating in the synagogue, and used their titles and tassels to separate "us" from "them." No wonder sparks flew when they met Jesus. Jesus couldn't have cared less about external appearance. In fact, He stripped Himself of all titles.

I once attended a meeting with people who were considered to be spiritual leaders within the city. I was saying hello and meeting people when I introduced myself to a man who introduced himself as Bishop Jones (not his real name). I replied with courtesy and addressed him by his first name. You would have thought I called his mother something awful. He loudly and quickly reminded me that his name was *Bishop* Jones and explained that he should not be addressed in any other manner. My first carnal thoughts were to use the same names Jesus used to describe some folks and a few of my own, but I didn't thankfully. I replayed that scene over and over in my mind many times after that day and think how sad it was that we had gotten so far away from the model Jesus gave us.

Jesus wanted to relate to man on an equal level. He used His power for the powerless. He loved the loveless and He served those who could not possibly return the favor. He said things like, "You will be great in my eyes when you demonstrate servanthood to the least deserving of those around you." You see, His focus was primarily on chickens eight, nine, and ten. Man! That was counter-cultural!

Today, Christ is asking us to bring humility and servanthood into our screwed up, dog-eat-dog, twisted society. Humility is the wisdom to know that we are each the same in the eyes of God — deeply flawed, yet extremely precious; none of us deserving of grace. Christ's blood was shed for Jeffrey Dalmer, Adolph Hitler, Mother Teresa, you, and me.

Understanding that this is at the root of humility, can you imagine the implications of actually applying this mentality to real life? What if everyone in the company treated everyone else like a VIP? What if the officers treated the clerical staff with great respect? What if doctors treated the nursing aides like the partners in health care that they really are? Imagine a political system where the politician's number-one motive was to serve the people. What if every husband stopped viewing himself as chicken number one with the right to peck at his wife who he has identified as chicken number two? Imagine the impact we could leave on peoples' lives if we all practiced preferential treatment for everyone!

How can it happen? It must begin in me and in you today. Don't ignore the reality of such a decision. Such behavior, though Christ-like, is costly. You don't buck the pecking order without a price. You see, anyone who truly loves experiences the pain of rejection, hatred, and anger first hand. Consider Jesus whose perfect love sent him to die on the cross.

Matthew 25:40 says, "The King will reply, 'I tell you the truth, whatever you did for one of the *least* of *these* brothers of mine, you did for me.'" Who are the least of these? They are whomever you have deemed them to be. Think about that statement for a moment. It's chickens eight, nine, and ten in your own eyes.

Look at the relationships and people around you today. Have you established a pecking order? Do you treat your boss with honor while dishonoring all below your level within the company? Do you treat your pastor with honor while dishonoring everyone else? Do you look around your church, measure yourself by others, and decide who is important and who is not? If so, then you have become part of a system that is totally un-Christ-like and will prevent you from ever descending into greatness and fulfilling God's purpose and plan for your life.

8 Downward Mobility: Keys to Greatness

"If there is any encouragement in Christ, if any consolation of love, if any fellowship with the Spirit, if any affection and mercy, fulfill my joy by thinking the same way, having the same love, sharing the same feelings, focusing on one goal. Do nothing out of rivalry or conceit, but in humility, consider others as more important than yourselves. Everyone should look out not only for his own interest, but also for the interests of others. Make your own attitude that of Christ Jesus who, existing in the form of God, did not consider equality with God as something to be used for His own advantage. Instead, He emptied Himself by assuming the form of a slave, taking on the likeness of men. And when He had come as a man in His external form, He humbled Himself by becoming obedient to the point of death, even to death on a cross. For this reason, God also highly exalted Him and gave Him the name

that is above every name so that at the name of Jesus, every knee should bow of those who are in Heaven and on earth and under the earth and every tongue confess that Jesus Christ is Lord, to the glory of God the Father."

Philippians 2:1-11
(Holman Christian Standard Bible)

Ours is a world of flux — one of seas that churn and change; one of seasons that slip one into the other; of lives that move in a steady motion from birth to death. We live in a world, it seems, that is in continual transformation where the only constant is change. In a world of change, evil is one thing you can count on. Evil is the net result of selfish, self-centered, self-serving people who care only about themselves. Maybe we aren't guilty of incinerating thousands of Jews, but how many times have we torn someone's heart out with our words? How many times have we wished someone out of existence — a spouse, a boss, an enemy — and allowed that wish to affect how we treated them and ultimately everyone around us.

Our words speak of grace, yet our actions often sting and wound. We claim to be pure and humble servants, then we complain that we get no applause. We pray for abundant life and yet chase after empty, self-indulgent dreams. The disease of evil is rooted in our hearts and there is no easy cure. Only Christ's blood, spilled from an innocent heart, is sufficient to overcome its power.

In our world, the word "down" is reserved for losers, cowards, and the bear market. It is a word to avoid or ignore and we certainly do not discuss it seriously. It is a word that colors whatever it touches. *Down* and out, *down*fall, *down*scale, *down*hill, *down*hearted, and *down*trodden — it has an awful ring to it, doesn't it? It is the opposite of up — a word our society not only cherishes but worships.

> *"Out of the heart comes evil thoughts, murderers, adulteries, fornications, thefts, false witness, and slanders."*
>
> *Matthew 15:19 (Holman Christian Standard Bible)*

"Up" is a word to admire, respect, and pursue. It is *up*scale, *up*wardly mobile, and *up*per class — the word of a chosen few. It is a word to describe the strong; a word that says, "I will rise against the odds, the crowd, and whatever or whomever gets in my way." Yes, "up" is clearly the word for greatness.

Into each heart is built a mechanism that craves self-promotion and advancement. Philippians 2 may be the most counter-cultural chapter in the Bible. It simply states that if you want to be great from God's perspective, then the direction you must go is down. It means demotion, anonymity, servanthood, downscaling, decreasing, losing, and dying.

Few Christians walk in the concept of downward mobility. Ask yourself, "When was the last time I downscaled, descended, or decreased so that the cause of Christ might be advanced?" How many of us have given sacrificially of our time and/or finances that the kingdom of God might move forward at an accelerated pace.

Joseph, after walking through many tests and being mistreated by many people, was made second man in the entire country. Instead of having a hard heart produced by a life of upward mobility, he had a God heart earned by living a life of downward mobility. Then and only then was he able to stand with hands full of bread in a famine-struck land.

Look around you right now. Do you see a spiritual famine in the lives of those around you — in the lives of family, co-workers, and, yes, even your church? They are looking to you and to me for the bread of life. Have we prepared our hearts to be silos of grain and life? Have we descended to the place that we will provide nourishment to those who have mistreated and overlooked us? The downward mobility, as modeled by Christ, will allow us to stand with hands full of bread to a dying, starving generation.

What's in your hands? Our Lord said, "I call Heaven and Earth to witness against you today: I place before you Life and Death, Blessing, and Curse. Choose life so that you and your children will live." (Deuteronomy 30:19, The Message: The Bible in Contemporary Language © 2002 by Eugene H. Peterson. All rights reserved.)

I believe this verse says we have the option of choosing life or death not only for ourselves but also for others. What will you choose? Joseph chose life for his nation, for his family, and even for his enemies. We see the ultimate fulfillment of this in Jesus our Lord as he also made the same choices. The King of Kings chose to be servant of all. The Author of Life chose death so that you and I might live life abundantly and inherit the kingdom of God.

Four Ways to Order More Copies

Online   Place your order online at www.soarhigher.com/BookStore.htm

E-mail   Place your order by e-mailing Soar with Eagles at carrie@soarhigher.com.

Telephone Call us at 479.636.7627 Monday through Friday
8:00 a.m. to 5:00 p.m. Central Time

Postal Mail Send your order to Soar with Eagles
1200 North Mallard Lane, Rogers, AR 72756 USA
Telephone: 479.636.7627

Soar with Eagles

A Publisher Driven by Vision and Purpose

Browse the selection of publications at www.soarhigher.com/BookStore.htm.

Order Form

Please send me _____ copies of the book at $9.95 each plus sales tax (applicable for Arkansas residents) plus shipping and handling.

Sales Tax

Please add 9.0% for Arkansas shipping addresses.

Shipping and Handling

USA: Add $4 for the first book and $2 for each additional book. International: $9 for the first book; $5 for each additional book.

Payment

❏ Check   Credit Card: ❏ Visa   ❏ MC   ❏ Amex

Card Number _____

Name on Card _____

Exp. Date _____

Signature _____

Your Information

Name _____

Address _____

City_____ State _____ Zip _____

Telephone _____

E-mail address _____

Book Stan Tyra at Your Next Conference

Stan Tyra is an accomplished speaker, leader, and motivator in both the corporate and faith-based arenas. He is an outstanding choice for a variety of events ranging from corporate meetings to churches and men's retreats.

Stan's warm, engaging style and his message of servant-leadership make him an excellent fit for an organization that believes in motivating and educating its leaders to bring out the best in their people.

Learn more about Stan and his programs by visiting the Speakers section at the Soar with Eagles website at www.soarhigher.com.